BEYOND THE RÍO GRANDE:
The Origins of El Paso, Texas

J. P. RALEY

Beyond the Río Grande: The Origins of El Paso, Texas
Written by JP Raley
© 2025. All Rights Reserved.

This book is dedicated to my better half who helps me in becoming the best version of myself, even after originally seeing each other over 34 years ago in Giessen, Germany. Thank you, Christine, for loving me as much as I love you. Here's to our future together, whole, and in love.

Introduction: A City at the Crossroads

El Paso, Texas, is more than a border town—it is a living testament to centuries of migration, conflict, and cultural blending. Nestled at the foot of the Franklin Mountains and straddling the Rio Grande, El Paso has always been a place where worlds meet. To understand its origins is to understand the story of North America itself: Indigenous resilience, Spanish conquest, Mexican independence, and American expansion all converge here.

Chapter 1: The River and the Desert

The desert does not give up its secrets easily. At first glance, the valley where El Paso now stands seems inhospitable: a stretch of ochre earth, jagged mountains rising like broken teeth, and a river that snakes through the land with moods as unpredictable as the people who would one day settle its banks. Yet for thousands of years, this place was not barren. It was alive.

The Rio Grande, known to the earliest peoples as a giver of life, carved a green ribbon through the desert. Cottonwoods leaned over its waters, their leaves shimmering like coins in the relentless sun. Along its floodplains, wild grasses grew tall, and the soil—darkened by centuries of silt—was fertile enough to sustain crops of maize, beans, and squash. To the north, the Franklin Mountains stood as silent sentinels, their granite faces catching the first light of dawn. To the south stretched the vast Chihuahuan Desert, a sea of mesquite, yucca, and creosote.

Here, long before the Spanish named it *El Paso del Norte*, the Manso, Suma, and Jumano peoples made their homes. They were not wanderers in a wasteland, as early European chroniclers sometimes imagined, but skilled stewards of the land. The Mansos planted along the riverbanks, their fields watered by ingenious irrigation ditches. The Jumanos, famed traders, carried salt, hides, and turquoise across hundreds of miles, linking the pueblos of New Mexico with the markets of central Mexico. The Sumas, hunters and gatherers, moved with the seasons, following the rhythms of the desert.

The river was not a boundary. It was a bridge. It connected communities, sustained life, and offered passage through the mountains. The valley was a crossroads long before Europeans ever dreamed of it.

But the desert also demanded respect. Summers scorched the land with temperatures that could blister skin in minutes. Winters brought sudden freezes, the mountains dusted with snow. Flash floods could sweep away entire villages, while droughts tested the endurance of even the most resilient. To live here was to live in balance with forces larger than oneself.

It was into this landscape that, in 1598, a column of weary Spaniards would stumble, searching for a way north. They would call it a "pass," but for those who had lived here for centuries, it was already something more: a home, a sanctuary, and a meeting place of worlds.

The story of El Paso begins not with conquest, but with the land itself—its river, its mountains, and the people who first learned to thrive in its embrace.

Chapter 2: The First Peoples

Long before the sound of Spanish hooves echoed across the desert, the valley of the Rio Grande was alive with voices, rituals, and the steady rhythm of life tied to the land. The people who lived here were not a single tribe, but a constellation of communities — the Manso, Suma, and Jumano — each with their own ways of surviving and thriving in the desert's embrace.

The Manso: Farmers of the River

The Manso people made their homes along the fertile banks of the Rio Grande. They were farmers, coaxing life from the soil with maize, beans, and squash — the "three sisters" that sustained countless Indigenous cultures across the Americas. Their villages were clusters of brush huts, simple yet suited to the climate, with roofs of willow and walls of reeds plastered with mud.

The river was their lifeline. They dug irrigation ditches to channel its waters into their fields, a practice that would later inspire Spanish settlers to expand the acequia system. Fishing, too, was central to their diet, and children learned early to cast nets into the current.

But the Manso were not only farmers. They were artisans, shaping pottery from river clay, and storytellers, passing down myths of creation and survival around evening fires. Their rituals honored the cycles of planting and harvest, the river's floods, and the spirits of the mountains that loomed above them.

The Suma: Wanderers of the Desert

To the east and north roamed the Suma, a semi-nomadic people who followed the shifting seasons. They hunted deer, rabbits, and bison when herds wandered close, and gathered mesquite beans, prickly pear, and agave. Their shelters were temporary, brush arbors that could be raised and abandoned as the desert demanded.

The Suma were masters of adaptation. In times of drought, they knew where to find hidden springs; in times of plenty, they traded with their neighbors. Their lives were shaped by movement, by the knowledge that survival in the desert meant never clinging too tightly to one place.

The Jumano: Traders of the Plains

The Jumano were the great middlemen of the Southwest, their influence stretching far beyond the El Paso valley. Known for their distinctive tattoos and body paint, they were recognized across the plains and deserts as skilled traders. They carried salt from the great lakes of West Texas, hides from the buffalo plains, and turquoise from the north, linking distant peoples in a web of commerce.

Some Jumanos lived in permanent villages, farming along rivers much like the Manso. Others roamed widely, guiding caravans across the desert. Their role as cultural brokers made them both respected and vulnerable, for they often stood at the crossroads of conflict between larger powers.

A Shared World

Though distinct, these peoples were bound together by the land. They gathered at the river for trade, for ceremonies, and for survival in times of hardship. Marriages linked families across tribal lines, and stories traveled as easily as goods.

The valley was not a wilderness waiting to be discovered — it was a homeland, rich with meaning. Every bend in the river, every cave in the mountains, every stand of mesquite carried a story. The people of the valley lived in dialogue with the land, shaping it and being shaped by it in return.

When the Spanish finally arrived in 1598, they would see only a fraction of this world. To them, the valley was a "pass," a gateway to the north. But to the Manso, Suma, and Jumano, it was already a center — a place where life had flourished for centuries, where the desert and the river met in fragile, enduring balance.

Chapter 3: Myths of the Valley

The desert was not silent to the first peoples of the Rio Grande. Every stone, every mountain peak, every bend in the river carried a story. To live here was to live inside a world of meaning, where the land itself spoke through myth and memory.

The Sacred Mountains

The Franklin Mountains, jagged and immovable, were more than stone. To the Manso, they were the bones of ancient giants, beings who had once walked the earth before the people. Their peaks were said to hold the spirits of ancestors, watching over the valley. Hunters whispered prayers before setting out, asking the mountains for safe passage and success.

The desert springs were equally sacred. The Suma told of a great serpent who slithered beneath the earth, its movements creating hidden pools of water. To find a spring was to find the serpent's blessing, and offerings of cornmeal or painted stones were left at the water's edge.

The River of Life

The Rio Grande was not merely a river — it was a living being. The Jumanos told stories of a woman clothed in turquoise who walked its banks at night, her hair flowing like water. She was the guardian of the river, and those who treated it with respect would find abundance in their fields and nets. But those who wasted its waters or polluted its banks risked her wrath, which came in the form of sudden floods.

Each spring, when the river swelled with snowmelt from the north, the Manso held ceremonies of renewal. Families gathered at the water's edge, singing songs that echoed across the valley, songs that told of the first planting, the first harvest, the first people.

Daily Life in the Valley

Life was not easy, but it was rich. Children learned early to weave baskets from yucca fibers, to grind maize on stone metates, to track rabbits across the desert floor. Women tended fields and prepared meals, their hands shaping tortillas from ground corn, their voices carrying lullabies that had been sung for generations.

Men hunted deer and bison when herds wandered close, their bows strung with sinew, their arrows tipped with obsidian. The hunt was not only survival but ceremony: before the kill, hunters painted their faces with red ochre, asking forgiveness from the spirit of the animal.

Trade was constant. The Jumanos, with their wide-ranging networks, brought salt, hides, and turquoise. In return, they carried away corn, pottery, and stories. Around campfires, tales were exchanged as readily as goods — tales of distant mountains, of gods who walked among men, of battles fought and alliances forged.

The World Before the Strangers

For centuries, this was the rhythm of life: planting and harvest, hunting and gathering, trade and ceremony. The people of the valley did not see themselves as isolated tribes but as part of a larger web, connected by the river and the desert.

Yet, in the late 16th century, whispers began to drift southward from the pueblos of New Mexico. Strange men had come from across the sea, clad in metal, riding beasts that seemed half-human, half-animal. They carried weapons that thundered like storms and demanded allegiance to a god unknown to the valley.

The Manso, Suma, and Jumano could not yet know how profoundly their world was about to change. But the signs were there: traders spoke of villages burned, of people taken as slaves, of new diseases that spread like fire through dry grass.

The valley still sang with its ancient stories, but a new story was approaching — one that would forever alter the meaning of the Pass of the North.

Chapter 4: The Coming of the Spanish

The desert shimmered with heat as the column of men, women, and animals wound its way northward. For weeks they had trudged across the Jornada del Muerto — the "Journey of the Dead Man" — a stretch of barren desert so unforgiving that even the most seasoned among them whispered prayers as they marched. Dust clung to their faces, lips cracked from thirst, and the sun seemed to press down with the weight of judgment.

At the head of the expedition rode Don Juan de Oñate, armored and resolute, his eyes fixed on the horizon. Behind him stretched a caravan of nearly five hundred souls: soldiers, settlers, priests, women, children, and enslaved Indigenous people forced into service. Herds of cattle and sheep stumbled along, their hooves raising clouds that blurred the line between earth and sky.

Then, at last, the land broke open. Before them lay a ribbon of green — the Rio Grande, glinting in the light like salvation itself. The weary travelers fell to their knees, some weeping, others crossing themselves, as the river promised what the desert had denied: water, life, and the possibility of a future.

On April 30, 1598, Oñate led his people into the river. Horses splashed, wagons creaked, and the current tugged at their legs as they crossed. On the far bank, they gathered in solemn ceremony. A great wooden cross was raised, and a mass was celebrated by Franciscan friars, their chants rising above the rush of the river.

But it was not only a religious act. Oñate declared the land for Spain, claiming it in the name of King Philip II. With words and ritual, the valley was bound into an empire that stretched across oceans. For the Indigenous peoples who had lived here for centuries, this moment marked the beginning of a new and turbulent era.

That evening, the expedition feasted. Game hunted along the river, fish pulled from its waters, and food carried from Mexico were shared in what some historians call the first true Thanksgiving on American soil — twenty-three years before the Pilgrims would land at

Plymouth Rock. Spaniards and Indigenous allies sat together, bound not by kinship but by necessity, giving thanks for survival in a land that had nearly claimed them.

The Rio Grande had become more than a river. It was now a border of worlds: the old and the new, the Indigenous and the European, the sacred and the imperial. The Pass of the North had entered history.

The Spaniards did not linger long in celebration. For Oñate and his men, the river was not only salvation but opportunity. To secure Spain's claim, they needed more than banners and proclamations — they needed permanence. That permanence would come in the form of missions.

The First Encounters

As the expedition settled along the riverbanks, they soon encountered the Manso people, whose villages dotted the fertile floodplains. The Mansos watched the newcomers with wary curiosity. To them, the Spaniards were unlike anything they had seen: men encased in metal, mounted on towering beasts, carrying weapons that spat fire and smoke.

Yet the first meetings were not marked by violence. The Mansos approached with offerings of food and water, gestures of hospitality in a land where survival often depended on generosity. In return, the Spaniards gave trinkets — beads, cloth, and small metal tools. Communication was halting, carried out through gestures and the few Indigenous allies who spoke fragments of related languages.

The Suma and Jumano peoples, more nomadic and wide-ranging, were slower to appear. But word of the strangers spread quickly across the desert. Traders carried tales of the newcomers' power, their strange rituals, and their insatiable hunger for land and allegiance.

The Missionary Vision

Among the expedition were Franciscan friars, men who saw the valley not only as a frontier of empire but as a frontier of faith. To them, the Indigenous peoples were souls to be saved, children in need of guidance. They envisioned adobe chapels rising along the river, bells calling the faithful to prayer, and fields tilled under the sign of the cross.

The first mission in the valley would not be built immediately — that would come in 1659 with = in what is now Ciudad Juárez — but the seeds were planted in these early encounters. The friars baptized willing Mansos, taught them prayers in halting Spanish, and promised protection under the banner of Christ.

For the Mansos, the friars' rituals were strange but not incomprehensible. They already lived in a world where the sacred infused the everyday, where rivers and mountains held spirits. To kneel before a cross was, at first, another gesture of respect to powerful beings. But beneath the surface, the encounter was more than ritual — it was the beginning of a profound transformation of their world.

Fragile Alliances

The Spaniards depended on the valley's peoples for food, guidance, and survival. The Mansos taught them where to find fish, how to dig for edible roots, and how to endure the desert's extremes. In return, the Spaniards offered iron tools, woven cloth, and the promise of alliance against rival tribes.

But the balance was fragile. The Spaniards demanded labor, tribute, and obedience to a distant king. The friars demanded conversion, the abandonment of old gods, and the reshaping of daily life around the rhythms of the church. For the Mansos, Sumas, and Jumanos, these demands would soon strain the bonds of hospitality.

A New Order Emerging

By the end of 1598, the valley was no longer the same. The river still flowed, the mountains still stood, and the people still sang their ancient songs — but now, alongside them, rose the sound of church bells and the crack of muskets.
The Spaniards had come not as passing travelers but as settlers, intent on remaking the valley in their image. The first encounters

had been cautious, even hopeful. But beneath the surface, tensions simmered. The Pass of the North had become a meeting ground of worlds — and the fragile peace would not last.

Chapter 5: The Pueblo Revolt and Refugees

The summer of 1680 brought fire to the north. Across the pueblos of New Mexico, long-simmering resentment against Spanish rule erupted into open rebellion. For decades, the Pueblo peoples had endured forced labor, suppression of their religious practices, and the relentless demands of missionaries who sought to erase their ancient traditions. Now, under the leadership of a Tewa man named Popé, they rose as one.

Spanish missions burned. Churches were torn down, their bells silenced, their crosses toppled. Priests were killed, soldiers driven out, and settlers forced to flee. For the first time in nearly a century of colonization, the Spanish were expelled from New Mexico.

The Flight South

The survivors fled southward, stumbling across the desert in desperate columns. Soldiers, friars, settlers, and Christianized Pueblo families — all sought refuge in the valley of the Rio Grande. By the time they reached El Paso del Norte, they were weary, hungry, and broken.

The valley, once a quiet frontier, suddenly swelled with thousands of refugees. The Mansos, who had long lived along the river, watched as their homeland was transformed overnight into a crowded sanctuary. The Spanish built temporary shelters, dug irrigation ditches, and began to organize the displaced into new communities.

A Refuge Becomes a Stronghold

El Paso del Norte became the northernmost outpost of Spanish power. Missions were established to anchor the refugees and to reassert control. Among them was the Mission of Nuestra Señora de Guadalupe, founded in 1659 but now elevated in importance as the spiritual and administrative heart of the region.

The friars worked feverishly to baptize and instruct the influx of Pueblo refugees, seeing in their suffering an opportunity to bind them more tightly to the church. For the Pueblo families who had fled south, life was complicated: they had resisted Spanish rule in their homelands, yet here they found themselves dependent on Spanish protection against enemies and starvation.

Tensions in the Valley

The sudden arrival of so many outsiders strained relations with the local tribes. The Mansos, Sumas, and Jumanos, already pressured by Spanish demands, now faced competition for land and resources. Some allied with the newcomers, hoping for protection or trade. Others resisted, raiding settlements or retreating deeper into the desert.

The Spanish, for their part, tightened their grip. They built presidios (forts) to defend against raids, expanded the mission system, and sought to weave the valley into the fabric of empire. What had once been a frontier crossroads was now a fortified refuge, a bulwark against both Indigenous resistance and rival European powers.

The Long Shadow of Revolt

The Pueblo Revolt reshaped the destiny of El Paso. What had been a marginal settlement became a center of Spanish authority, a staging ground for the eventual reconquest of New Mexico in 1692. The valley's identity as a place of refuge, resilience, and cultural blending was forged in these years of upheaval.

For the Indigenous peoples of the valley, however, the cost was high. Their lands were crowded with strangers, their autonomy eroded, their traditions increasingly suppressed. Yet they endured, adapting as they always had, finding ways to preserve fragments of their world beneath the weight of empire.

The Pass of the North had become more than a crossing. It was now a crucible — a place where cultures collided, where survival demanded compromise, and where the future of the borderlands was being written in blood, faith, and resilience.

A Valley Transformed

The arrival of thousands of refugees after 1680 did more than swell the population — it transformed the very identity of the valley. What had once been a relatively quiet frontier of scattered Manso villages and a handful of Spanish settlers became a bustling, contested hub. Adobe shelters multiplied along the riverbanks, irrigation ditches spread outward, and the sound of hammers and bells echoed where once only the wind and river spoke.

The Manso people, who had long lived along the Rio Grande, suddenly found themselves outnumbered in their own homeland. Some were drawn into the orbit of the missions, baptized and folded into the new communities. Others resisted, retreating into the desert or allying with the Suma and Apache raiders who harried the Spanish.

The Missions as Anchors

The Spanish response to crisis was to build. Missions became the anchors of their presence, both spiritual and political. The Mission of Nuestra Señora de Guadalupe, founded in 1659, now stood at the heart of El Paso del Norte, its adobe walls thick and cool against the desert sun. Around it clustered new settlements: San Lorenzo, Senecú, Ysleta, and Socorro, each established to house displaced Pueblo families and their Franciscan overseers.

Life in these mission communities was regimented. Days began with the ringing of bells, calling the faithful to mass. Fields were worked communally under the friars' supervision, with maize, wheat, and grapes cultivated in the fertile floodplain. Children were taught prayers in Spanish and Latin, their native languages discouraged, their dances and ceremonies forbidden.

Yet beneath the surface, the old traditions endured. Pueblo families whispered their prayers to the kachinas in secret, painted symbols on pottery that carried hidden meanings, and passed down stories of the revolt as a reminder of resistance. The missions were not only places of conversion but also sites of quiet defiance.

A Frontier Under Siege

The valley was not free from danger. To the north, the Pueblo peoples who had expelled the Spanish remained independent for more than a decade, a constant reminder of what resistance could achieve. To the east and west, Apache raiders struck at settlements, seizing livestock and goods. The Spanish built presidios to defend their fragile foothold, but the frontier remained volatile.

For the refugees, life was precarious. They had escaped the violence of the revolt only to find themselves caught between Spanish demands and the harsh realities of the desert borderlands. Hunger, disease, and raids were constant threats. Yet the communities endured, bound together by necessity and the hope of survival.

The Seeds of a Borderland Identity

In these years, the valley of El Paso del Norte began to take on the character that would define it for centuries: a place of convergence and resilience. Spanish settlers, Pueblo refugees, Mansos, Sumas, and later Apaches all lived in uneasy proximity, their lives intertwined by trade, conflict, and necessity.

The Pueblo Revolt had forced the Spanish south, but it had also ensured that El Paso would never again be a marginal outpost. It was now a center of colonial life, a stronghold from which Spain would eventually reconquer New Mexico in 1692.

For the Indigenous peoples of the valley, however, the cost was profound. Their lands were reshaped, their traditions suppressed, their autonomy eroded. Yet they endured, carrying their stories forward, adapting to the new order while never fully surrendering the old.

The Pass of the North had become a crucible — and from its fires, a new borderland identity was forged.

Chapter 6: Life on the Edge of Empire

The valley of El Paso del Norte in the late 17th and early 18th centuries was a place of contrasts. On the surface, it bore the marks of Spanish order: adobe missions rising above the riverbanks, bells tolling the hours of prayer, fields of maize and wheat stretching across the floodplain. Yet beneath this veneer of stability lay a world of uncertainty, where survival depended on fragile alliances, constant vigilance, and the endurance of cultures that refused to vanish.

The Mission Communities

By the early 1700s, the valley was dotted with mission settlements: Ysleta, Socorro, Senecú, San Lorenzo, and the great Guadalupe Mission at the heart of El Paso del Norte. Each was home to a mix of peoples — Pueblo refugees, Mansos, Sumas, and a growing number of mestizo families born of Spanish and Indigenous unions.

Life in these communities followed a strict rhythm. The day began with the ringing of bells, calling residents to mass. Afterward, men and women worked the fields, tending maize, beans, wheat, and vineyards introduced by the Spaniards. Children learned catechism from the friars, their native languages discouraged, their dances and ceremonies forbidden. Yet in the privacy of homes and in the quiet of the desert, old traditions endured.

The Frontier Economy

The valley's economy was a blend of old and new. Indigenous irrigation techniques were expanded into acequias, communal canals that carried river water to the fields. Spanish livestock — cattle, sheep, and horses — grazed on the plains, transforming the landscape and the diet of the people. Trade caravans moved south to Chihuahua and north toward Santa Fe, carrying hides, salt, and agricultural goods.

But the frontier was never secure. Apache raids were a constant threat, striking at herds and settlements. The presidios — small forts manned by Spanish soldiers — offered some protection, but the valley remained vulnerable. Every harvest was shadowed by the possibility of loss.

A Blended Culture

Despite the hardships, a unique culture began to take shape. Spanish hymns mingled with Indigenous chants; adobe churches stood beside traditional brush huts; and families wove together traditions from both worlds. Festivals blended Catholic saints' days with older seasonal rituals, creating celebrations that were neither wholly Spanish nor wholly Indigenous, but something new.

Food, too, told the story of blending: maize tortillas alongside wheat bread, chile peppers mixed with European herbs, goats' milk cheese paired with beans and squash. The valley was becoming a place where cultures did not simply collide but intertwined, creating a borderland identity that would endure for centuries.

The Weight of Empire

For all its blending, El Paso del Norte remained firmly under the shadow of empire. Taxes, tribute, and labor demands tied the valley to distant authorities in Mexico City and Madrid. The friars saw themselves as guardians of souls, but also as agents of control. The people of the valley lived with the knowledge that their lives were shaped not only by the desert and the river, but by decisions made in faraway halls of power.

And yet, despite the weight of empire, the valley endured. Families planted, harvested, prayed, and told stories. Children grew up speaking words from two worlds. The river flowed, the mountains stood, and life continued on the edge of empire — precarious, resilient, and deeply human.

The Fragile Frontier

To live in El Paso del Norte in the 17th and 18th centuries was to live in a place both central and marginal. Central, because the valley had become the northernmost stronghold of Spanish power after the Pueblo Revolt; marginal, because it was still a frontier, vulnerable to raids, droughts, and the shifting loyalties of its peoples. The Spanish crown claimed the land, but the desert never fully yielded.

The Missions as Engines of Change

The missions were more than churches — they were engines of cultural transformation. Each mission settlement was carefully organized:

- The church stood at the center, its adobe walls thick and cool, its altar adorned with painted saints.
- The plaza spread before it, a gathering place for markets, festivals, and proclamations.
- The fields stretched outward, watered by acequias, where Pueblo refugees and local tribes labored under the friars' supervision.

The friars sought to reshape every aspect of life. They taught European farming techniques, introduced livestock, and enforced Catholic rituals. Baptisms, marriages, and burials were recorded in parish books, binding Indigenous families into the bureaucratic fabric of empire.

Yet the people of the valley were not passive recipients. They adapted, resisted, and blended. Old songs were sung quietly at night, dances performed in secret, and pottery designs carried symbols of gods the friars thought forgotten. The missions became places of both conversion and quiet defiance.

The Presidio and the Sword

If the friars wielded the cross, the soldiers wielded the sword. The presidios — small forts manned by Spanish troops — were meant to defend the valley against Apache raids and to project Spanish authority. Soldiers patrolled the desert, escorted caravans, and enforced tribute.

But presidio life was harsh. Supplies were scarce, pay was often delayed, and soldiers' families lived in poverty. Many turned to trade or farming to survive, blurring the line between soldier and settler. Over time, presidio communities became as much a part of the valley as the missions, their children growing up speaking both Spanish and Indigenous tongues.

The Apache Threat

The greatest danger came from the Apache, whose raids defined frontier life. To the Apache, the arrival of Spanish settlers and their livestock was both a threat and an opportunity. Raids brought horses, cattle, and goods, but also provoked bloody reprisals.

For the people of El Paso del Norte, the threat of attack was constant. Herds had to be guarded, fields watched, and travelers moved in groups. Stories of raids — sudden, violent, and devastating — circulated through the valley, shaping a culture of vigilance. Yet even here, the lines were not absolute. Trade and negotiation sometimes tempered conflict, and Apache captives were occasionally absorbed into mission communities, further blending the valley's population.

Daily Rhythms of Survival

Despite the dangers, life followed its rhythms.

- Agriculture: Families rose with the sun to tend maize, beans, wheat, and vineyards.

Harvest festivals blended Catholic saints' days with older seasonal rituals.
- Crafts and trade: Women wove cloth on looms, men shaped tools from iron, and pottery carried both Spanish and Indigenous designs. Caravans carried goods south to Chihuahua and north toward Santa Fe, linking the valley to distant markets.
- Faith and festivity: The calendar was punctuated by feast days — processions for the Virgin, dances in the plaza, fireworks that lit the desert sky. These celebrations were both religious and communal, moments when the hardships of frontier life gave way to joy.

A Borderland Identity Emerges

By the 18th century, El Paso del Norte was no longer simply a Spanish outpost. It was a borderland society, shaped by the blending of cultures. Spanish settlers, Pueblo refugees, Mansos, Sumas, mestizos, and even Apache captives lived side by side, their lives intertwined by necessity.

The people of the valley spoke in many tongues, cooked with many traditions, and prayed to many gods — some openly, some in secret. They were subjects of the Spanish crown, but their identity was something more complex: a frontier people, resilient, adaptive, and deeply tied to the land.

The Edge of Empire

For all its blending, El Paso del Norte remained precarious. Distant authorities in Mexico City demanded tribute and loyalty but offered little protection. The friars dreamed of souls saved, the soldiers dreamed of glory, and the settlers dreamed of stability. Yet the desert had its own demands, and the people of the valley learned to live not by the dictates of empire alone, but by the rhythms of the river, the mountains, and the ever-present threat of change.

El Paso del Norte was not yet the city it would become, but its character was already clear: a place of convergence, resilience, and survival — a community forged on the edge of empire.

Chapter 7: Independence and instability, 1821–1848

The valley had learned to live under distant kings. In 1821, the king vanished. Mexico declared its independence, and El Paso del Norte—long a northern outpost of New Spain—found itself under a new flag with old problems. The bells still rang at Guadalupe; the river still flooded and receded; caravans still creaked south to Chihuahua and north toward the plazas of Santa Fe. But the scaffolding of empire—laws, garrisons, stipends—was suddenly replaced by promises and uncertainty. Independence carried hope; the frontier answered with hard questions.

A new nation, old realities

The first years after independence were filled with proclamations and paper. Mexico City sent governors to Chihuahua, decrees to the presidios, and plans for secularization to missions that had anchored the valley for generations. In El Paso del Norte, the meaning of independence was measured in grain, livestock, and the reliability of escorts on dangerous roads, not in slogans. Local alcaldes balanced the books; friars negotiated their futures; merchants watched exchange rates like the sky for signs of weather.

- Secularization begins: Mexico's liberal currents pressed missions to yield land and authority to civil society. Parish life continued at Guadalupe, but community fields and obligations shifted under new rules.
- Garrisons thin out: Military stipends lagged, patrols grew infrequent, and presidios improvised—trading, farming, and bargaining to keep watch on a vast horizon.
- Paper meets desert: Laws arrived faster than resources. On the ground, custom and necessity still ruled.

Trade arteries and the rise of the customs house

If the crown's chains loosened, commerce's threads tightened. The Chihuahua Trail through El Paso del Norte became a lifeline for the northern economy: wool, hides, copper, and silver moved south; cloth, tools, and luxuries moved north. The customs house—small, dusty, indispensable—stood between ambition and ruin.

- **Caravans and credit:** Merchants advanced goods on credit to ranchers and farmers; debts were settled after harvests or in livestock, sometimes in lawsuits that lingered longer than seasons.
- **Smuggling as survival:** Tariffs fluctuated with politics, but hunger and opportunity remained constant. Smuggling was not a romance—it was arithmetic: risk versus reward on moonless nights along the river.
- **Networks of trust:** Deals were sealed with handshakes, sealed again with witnesses, sealed a third time with shared hardship on the trail. Reputation traveled faster than wagons.

The frontier of conflict: Comanche, Apache, and negotiation

Independence did not change the wind's direction or the routes of raiders. Apache bands tested settlements near the valley's margins; Comanche raiding circuits pressed deeper into Chihuahua. The response was uneven: sometimes lances and muskets, sometimes gifts and parleys, often both.

- **Defensive rings:** Watchtowers rose along acequias; herds grazed closer to clustered homes; armed escorts shadowed harvests.
- **Parley and tribute:** Pragmatism bred negotiations—food, tools, and livestock exchanged for quiet seasons. The line between treaty and protection payment blurred in sand.
- **Captives and kin:** Raids ended in blood and bargains. Captives were ransomed, adopted, or integrated—another layer in the valley's tangled kinship.

Family rhythms under a shifting sky

Independence filtered into the home through small things: a new saint's day procession with republican banners, a ledger written in a different hand, a son absent on a caravan, a daughter marrying across language. The river kept time with floods; families kept time with planting, weddings, and funerals.

- Acequia governance: Water commissioners—elected, respected, feared—measured and meted flow. A dry season taught humility; a wet season taught patience.
- Women's work, women's wealth: Looms, kitchens, and gardens spun value into cloth and meals; dowries—land, tools, cattle—anchored alliances.
- Health and hazard: Cholera rode the trade routes; fevers came with heat; midwives and curanderas stitched health from herbs, prayer, and knowledge older than republics.

The Texas Revolution and the distant thunder

When Texas rebelled in 1835–1836, the thunder was far to the east. In El Paso del Norte, news arrived late and left early. The valley remained under Chihuahua's orbit, but maps began to matter more. Anglo merchants appeared more often; languages braided in markets; rumors of new borders mixed with old realities.

- Military movement at margins: Troops and supplies shifted through the north, more seen as road dust than as security.
- Price shocks and scarcity: The conflict jostled trade, spiking prices for munitions and staples; merchants hedged in silver and patience.
- A wary curiosity: Texans were a story told secondhand—first as rebels, then as neighbors, someday perhaps as officials. For the valley, they were another variable.

A Distant Rebellion, a Nearby Anxiety

When the Texas Revolution erupted in 1835, El Paso del Norte was far from the battlefields of Gonzales, San Jacinto, and the Alamo. Yet distance did not mean detachment. The valley's merchants, ranchers, and officials watched events with unease. The rebellion was not simply a local uprising — it was a challenge to Mexican sovereignty, and its outcome would redraw the map of the north.

- Rumors and reports: News traveled slowly, carried by traders and soldiers. Stories of

Anglo settlers defying Mexican law, of massacres and victories, reached El Paso weeks or months after the fact, often distorted by distance.
- Fear of contagion: Officials in Chihuahua worried that rebellion might spread. If Anglo settlers could defy Mexico in Texas, what would stop other frontier communities from asserting independence?
- Merchants' dilemma: Traders in El Paso had long dealt with Anglo merchants along the Santa Fe Trail. Now, those same Anglos were citizens of a breakaway republic. Commerce continued, but with suspicion.

The Republic of Texas and the Rio Grande Claim

After Texas declared independence in 1836, its leaders claimed the Rio Grande as the republic's southern boundary. On paper, this meant that El Paso del Norte — hundreds of miles west of San Antonio — was part of Texas. In reality, Mexican authority remained unchallenged in the valley.

- A claim without control: The Republic of Texas never established effective governance in El Paso. No Texan officials arrived, no taxes were collected, no garrisons were stationed.
- Symbolic tension: For El Pasoans, the claim was a reminder that their valley was now on the edge of two nations' ambitions. Maps in Austin and Washington showed El Paso as Texan; maps in Mexico City showed it as Chihuahua.
- Local perspective: To the people of the valley, the claim was almost abstract. Their lives were tied to Chihuahua's markets, Mexico's laws, and the river's cycles. Yet the shadow of Texas loomed larger with each passing year.

Trade, Smuggling, and Shifting Loyalties

The creation of the Republic of Texas disrupted established trade routes. Goods that once flowed freely between Chihuahua and the Anglo settlements of the east now crossed a contested border.

- Smuggling networks: Tariffs and blockades encouraged smuggling. El Paso merchants quietly moved goods northward into Texas, while Texan traders slipped south with contraband.
- Cultural crossings: Anglo traders began appearing more frequently in El Paso, bringing English words, Protestant Bibles, and new goods. Some families welcomed the commerce; others saw it as a threat to tradition.
- A divided horizon: For the first time, El Pasoans began to imagine their future not only as part of Mexico, but also in relation to the growing Anglo presence to the east.

The Mexican nation in turbulence

Independence did not guarantee stability. Federalists and centralists contested Mexico's soul; governors turned over; decrees reversed. In El Paso del Norte, turbulence translated into interrupted patrols, unpaid soldiers, and pragmatic improvisation.

- Local councils as ballast: Cabildos mediated disputes, apportioned water, levied small

taxes, and kept records that outlasted governors.
- **Church and state recalibrated:** Parish priests navigated secular laws, marriages, and property claims with pastoral stubbornness; sacraments outlived policy.
- **Endurance by habit:** When politics faltered, people planted anyway. A well-dug ditch could survive three administrations.

War on the horizon: 1846–1848

By 1846, war was no longer rumor as the uneasy balance collapsed in 1846, when the United States annexed Texas and war broke out with Mexico. For El Paso del Norte, the war was both distant and immediate. The United States marched into northern Mexico; battles flared in places whose names the valley would know: Palo Alto, Monterrey, Buena Vista. Soldiers passed through the north; fear and profit traveled together. El Paso del Norte counted flour, tallied livestock, and waited.

- **Supply and spectacle:** Military caravans demanded fodder, provisions, guides. Some

families prospered supplying armies; others hid herds beyond the river's bends.
- A fragile neutrality: Many tried to stand aside—too small to join, too exposed to resist—keeping heads down while keeping ledgers open.

- Military passage: U.S. troops marched through northern Mexico, and though El Paso was spared major battles, the presence of armies disrupted trade and strained resources.
- Divided loyalties: Some merchants quietly profited by supplying U.S. forces; others remained staunchly loyal to Mexico. Families were caught between pragmatism and patriotism.
- The Treaty of Guadalupe Hidalgo (1848): When the war ended, the treaty fixed the Rio Grande as the border. For El Paso, this was the most profound change of all. The river that had always been a lifeline now became a line of division.
- The treaty's long shadow: In 1848, the Treaty of Guadalupe Hidalgo redrew the map. The Rio Grande became an international boundary for much of the north; the valley's single community faced a cartographer's knife.

El Paso Split in Two

The treaty's cartographers drew a line that split the valley. On the south bank remained El Paso del Norte (today Ciudad Juárez), still part of Mexico. On the north bank, the small settlements of Ysleta, Socorro, and San Elizario were now part of the United States, within the state of Texas.

- Families divided: Kin who had lived within walking distance were suddenly citizens of different nations.
- Dual identities: Many residents refused to see themselves as wholly Mexican or wholly Texan. They continued to trade, marry, and worship across the river, ignoring the border when possible.
- The birth of El Paso, Texas: Though still small, the north-bank settlements would grow into the city of El Paso, Texas, while El Paso del Norte remained the Mexican counterpart. The valley was now two cities, one community split by politics.

A river becomes a line

For centuries, the river had been a corridor. Now it was a demarcation. El Paso del Norte and its north-bank settlements found themselves looking across at what would soon be called El Paso, Texas. Families discovered that kin could be foreign; contracts learned to cross borders.

- Citizenship by current: A home's location decided nationality, often more than language or loyalty. Papers multiplied; oaths changed; identities adjusted without surrender.
- Two regimes, one market: Tariffs diverged, laws shifted, but demand remained. Smugglers refined their calculus; merchants learned both legal systems; notaries earned their keep.
- Continuity beneath division: Weddings still crossed water; funerals still gathered both banks; stories still ignored lines.

The valley at 1848: an inventory of resilience

Independence had brought hopes and strain, profits and losses, raids and remedies. The treaty brought a border. Yet the essentials endured: acequias ran; bells tolled; markets opened at dawn; elders told history in kitchens as thick-walled as memory.

- What changed: Flags, tariffs, patrol routes, and the language of officials.
- What persisted: Water rights customs, kin networks, seasonal rhythms, and a habit of making peace with the possible.
- What emerged: A borderland identity strong enough to hold contradiction—Mexican and American, Indigenous and Spanish, merchant and farmer—without shattering.

The pass had always been a place of meeting. Independence and instability taught it to be a place of staying: rooted in land, flexible in law, measured by survival rather than slogans. In the years to come, rails would lay iron across the desert, and the line would be policed as never before. But the valley's answer would remain the same: plant, trade, endure—and refuse to forget who belonged to both banks of the river.

A Border Forged in Instability

Between 1835 and 1848, El Paso del Norte lived through a transformation it did not choose. Texas independence, the Republic's claim to the Rio Grande, and the Mexican-American War turned the valley from a remote frontier into a borderland of nations.

For centuries, the river had been a bridge. Now it was a boundary. Yet the people of El Paso adapted, as they always had. They traded across the line, married across the line, and prayed across the line. The border was real, but life in the valley refused to be contained by it.

Chapter 8: Two Cities, One Valley

A River Divides, a Community Endures

In 1848, the Treaty of Guadalupe Hidalgo transformed the Rio Grande from a lifeline into a boundary. On the north bank, the small settlements of Ysleta, Socorro, and San Elizario were absorbed into the United States, soon joined by a growing town that would take the name El Paso, Texas. On the south bank, the historic heart of the valley — El Paso del Norte — remained part of Mexico.

Though the treaty drew a line, the people of the valley did not suddenly become strangers. Families continued to cross the river for weddings, funerals, and trade. Merchants carried goods back and forth, often ignoring tariffs and customs officials. The river was a border on maps, but in daily life it remained a bridge.

Divergent Paths of Growth

Despite their shared roots, the two communities began to develop along different trajectories.

- **El Paso, Texas**:
  - Benefited from the arrival of the railroads in the 1880s, which connected it to the booming markets of the United States.
  - Attracted Anglo settlers, entrepreneurs, and soldiers, transforming it into a bustling frontier city.
  - Became a hub for cattle ranching, mining, and later, cross-border trade.
- El Paso del Norte (Mexico):
  - Remained the older, more established settlement, with its missions, plazas, and colonial traditions.
  - Served as a cultural and political center for northern Chihuahua.
  - Became a refuge for exiles, revolutionaries, and migrants moving northward.

The two cities looked across the river at one another, each reflecting a different national destiny, yet bound by geography and kinship.

The Name Change: From El Paso del Norte to Ciudad Juárez

By the mid-19th century, the name *El Paso del Norte* carried centuries of history. But in 1888, the Mexican government officially renamed the city Ciudad Juárez, in honor of Benito Juárez, the revered Mexican president who had once taken refuge there.

- Why the change?
  - During the French Intervention (1862–1867), when Emperor Maximilian ruled Mexico with French support, Benito Juárez led the republican resistance.
  - In 1865, Juárez and his government fled north, establishing their seat of power in El Paso del Norte for a time. From here, he issued decrees, rallied support, and symbolized Mexican resilience.
  - By renaming the city in 1888, Mexico honored Juárez's legacy and cemented the valley's role in the defense of the republic.
- Symbolism of the name:
  - The change distinguished the Mexican city from its U.S. counterpart, which was rapidly growing under the name El Paso.

- It asserted Mexican identity at a time when U.S. influence in the borderlands was expanding.
- It transformed the city into a living monument to Juárez, the champion of Mexican sovereignty and reform.

Two Cities, One Valley

By the end of the 19th century, the valley was home to El Paso, Texas, looked northward, tied to the United States' economy and culture. Ciudad Juárez looked southward, rooted in Mexican politics and traditions. Yet the river between them was not a wall but a thread, binding their histories together.

- Workers crossed daily for jobs.
- Families straddled both sides of the border.
- Revolutions, wars, and economic booms would ripple across the river, shaping both cities in tandem.

The Pass of the North had become a borderland in the truest sense: two nations, two cities, one valley.

Iron Rails Across the Desert

The arrival of the railroads in the 1880s transformed the valley more than any event since the drawing of the border. For centuries, El Paso del Norte had been a frontier town, its lifeblood tied to mule caravans and dusty trade routes. Suddenly, steel rails stitched the desert to the wider world.

- In 1881, the Southern Pacific Railroad reached El Paso, Texas, linking it westward to California.
- The Atchison, Topeka & Santa Fe Railway soon followed, connecting El Paso to the Midwest and beyond.
- On the Mexican side, the Mexican Central Railway reached El Paso del Norte in 1884, tying the city to Chihuahua and Mexico City.

The valley was no longer isolated. It was a crossroads of nations, a hub where goods, people, and ideas flowed in both directions.

El Paso, Texas: From Frontier Town to Boom City

The railroad turned El Paso, Texas, from a dusty settlement into a booming city almost overnight.

- Population explosion: In 1880, El Paso had fewer than 1,000 residents. By 1890, it had more than 10,000, and by 1910, nearly 40,000.
- Economic growth: Railroads brought cattle, copper, and cotton to market. Saloons, hotels, and businesses sprang up along the tracks.
- A new identity: El Paso became known as the "Six-Shooter Capital," a frontier city of gamblers, gunfighters, and entrepreneurs. Yet beneath the rough edges, it was also a city of ambition, eager to claim its place in the modern American West.

El Paso del Norte: Tradition Meets Transformation

On the south bank, El Paso del Norte felt the same surge of energy. The Mexican Central Railway brought goods and migrants from the interior of Mexico, fueling growth.

- Urban expansion: Streets were widened, plazas modernized, and new businesses

opened to serve both locals and cross-border visitors.
- Cultural vibrancy: The city retained its colonial heart — adobe churches, shaded plazas, and traditional markets — but now pulsed with the energy of modern commerce.
- Renaming to Ciudad Juárez (1888): To honor Benito Juárez, who had made the city his seat of government during the French Intervention, El Paso del Norte was renamed Ciudad Juárez. The new name symbolized Mexican pride and sovereignty, distinguishing it from its northern twin.

Two Cities, One Economy

Though divided by the Rio Grande, the two cities were inseparable.

- Labor and migration: Mexican workers crossed daily into El Paso, Texas, to build railroads, work in smelters, and tend ranches. Many returned home each night to Ciudad Juárez, carrying wages that sustained families and fueled local markets.
- Commerce and smuggling: Goods flowed across the border legally and illegally. Tariffs and customs houses mattered less than the

river's shallow crossings, where merchants and smugglers alike carried flour, liquor, and textiles.
- Shared vices, shared profits: El Paso's saloons and gambling halls drew crowds from both sides. When prohibitionist laws tightened in Texas, Ciudad Juárez became the playground, offering cantinas, bullfights, and entertainment that Americans eagerly consumed.

A Shared Destiny

By the dawn of the 20th century, El Paso and Ciudad Juárez were no longer frontier outposts. They were twin cities, each reflecting the character of its nation but bound together by geography and necessity.

- El Paso, Texas looked northward, tied to the United States' economy, law, and culture.
- Ciudad Juárez looked southward, rooted in Mexican politics and traditions.
- Yet both looked across the river at one another, their fates intertwined.

When revolution swept Mexico in 1910, El Paso became a refuge for exiles and a staging ground for revolutionaries. When the U.S. economy boomed, Ciudad Juárez thrived on cross-border trade and tourism. When one city suffered, the other felt the tremors.

The railroad had done more than bring prosperity. It had bound the two cities into a single organism, two halves of one valley, destined to share triumphs and tragedies alike.

A Military Outpost on the Border

The Treaty of Guadalupe Hidalgo in 1848 not only redrew the map of the valley but also brought the U.S. Army to its banks. To secure the newly established border and protect settlers, the Army established a small outpost near El Paso, Texas. This was the seed of what would become Fort Bliss.

At first, the post was little more than a cluster of adobe buildings and tents, manned by a handful of soldiers tasked with patrolling the Rio Grande and deterring Apache raids. Yet its presence signaled something larger: the United States intended to hold this frontier, not merely claim it on paper.

Naming Fort Bliss (1854)

In 1854, the outpost was officially named Fort Bliss, in honor of Colonel William Wallace Smith Bliss, a distinguished officer who had served as chief of staff to General Zachary Taylor during the Mexican–American War. The naming was symbolic — a reminder that the fort's existence was rooted in the war that had divided the valley into two nations.

Over the decades, Fort Bliss would grow in size and importance. It became not only a military installation but also a stabilizing presence in a region defined by shifting borders, raids, and revolutions. Soldiers stationed there built roads, guarded caravans, and provided a sense of permanence to the fledgling city of El Paso.

Fort Bliss and the Twin Cities

As El Paso and El Paso del Norte (later Ciudad Juárez) developed side by side, Fort Bliss became a constant presence in the background. Its soldiers mingled in the saloons of El Paso, its payroll supported local businesses, and its defenses reassured settlers who feared raids or unrest.

The fort also symbolized the growing Americanization of the north bank. While Ciudad Juárez remained tied to Mexico's traditions and politics, El Paso's identity was increasingly shaped by the U.S. Army's presence and the sense of security it provided.

Foreshadowing Revolution

By the early 20th century, Fort Bliss had grown into one of the most important military posts in the Southwest. Its role would expand dramatically during the Mexican Revolution (1910–1920), when the U.S. Army used it as a staging ground for border patrols, intelligence gathering, and even the Punitive Expedition against Pancho Villa in 1916.

Thus, the establishment of Fort Bliss in 1848 was more than a military footnote. It was the beginning of a story that would glide seamlessly into the valley's revolutionary era. The fort's adobe walls and parade grounds would witness not only the taming of a frontier but also the turbulence of international conflict, making it a thread that tied the valley's past to its future.

Chapter 9: Law and Disorder

A Frontier in Transition

By the 1890s, the twin cities of El Paso, Texas, and Ciudad Juárez, Mexico had become something new: not sleepy frontier towns, not yet modern metropolises, but boomtowns. The railroad had brought prosperity, but prosperity came with chaos. The valley was a magnet for fortune-seekers, outlaws, gamblers, and entrepreneurs. It was a place where fortunes could be made overnight — and lives could be lost just as quickly.

El Paso, Texas, in particular, earned a reputation as one of the wildest towns in the American West. Newspapers called it the "Six-Shooter Capital," a city where saloons outnumbered churches and where disputes were often settled not in courtrooms but in the dusty streets.

Saloons, Gambling, and Vice

The railroad brought not only goods and settlers but also vice industries that thrived on the constant flow of travelers.

- Saloons lined El Paso's main streets, offering whiskey, poker, and companionship. By 1900, there were more than 100 saloons in the city, many open around the clock.
- Gambling halls flourished, attracting cowboys, miners, and railroad men eager to test their luck. Roulette wheels spun, dice clattered, and fortunes changed hands in minutes.
- Prostitution was openly tolerated in El Paso's "red-light district," known as the Utah Street Reservation, where brothels operated under a system of regulation and taxation.

Across the river, Ciudad Juárez mirrored and magnified these industries. Mexican authorities, less constrained by U.S. reform movements, allowed bullfights, cockfights, and cantinas to flourish. When Texas passed stricter laws on gambling and alcohol, Americans simply crossed the bridge to Juárez, where the party continued.

Lawmen and Outlaws

With vice came violence. El Paso's streets were notorious for gunfights, robberies, and murders.

- Famed gunmen like Dallas Stoudenmire, who served as El Paso's marshal in the 1880s, became legends for their quick tempers and quicker draws. Stoudenmire's "Four Dead in Five Seconds" gunfight cemented the city's reputation for bloodshed.
- Outlaws and fugitives found refuge in the valley, slipping across the river to evade authorities. The international border made law enforcement complicated; a man wanted in Texas could vanish into Juárez, and vice versa.
- Corruption was rampant. Lawmen often had ties to saloon owners or gambling bosses, blurring the line between order and disorder.

A City of Contradictions

Despite its reputation for lawlessness, El Paso was also a city of ambition. Civic leaders built schools, courthouses, and rail depots. Churches rose alongside saloons, and newspapers debated the city's future.

Respectable families lived just blocks away from gambling dens, and businessmen who condemned vice by day often profited from it by night.

Ciudad Juárez, too, embodied contradiction. It was both a traditional Mexican town, with its colonial plaza and adobe homes, and a modern border city catering to American tourists. Its economy thrived on cross-border vice, yet its identity was deeply tied to Mexican nationalism, especially after adopting the name of Benito Juárez in 1888.

The Calm Before the Storm

By the first decade of the 20th century, the valley was booming. Railroads, ranching, mining, and trade fueled growth. El Paso's population soared, and Ciudad Juárez prospered from cross-border commerce and tourism. Yet beneath the prosperity lay tension.

- In Mexico, discontent simmered under the long rule of Porfirio Díaz, whose modernization policies enriched elites but left many poor and landless.

- In El Paso, reformers began pushing back against the city's reputation for vice, clashing with those who profited from it.
- The border itself became a stage for smuggling, political intrigue, and revolutionary whispers.

The boomtown years were a time of law and disorder, of opportunity and danger, of prosperity built on fragile foundations. Soon, the valley would be swept into a storm far greater than saloon brawls or railroad disputes. The Mexican Revolution of 1910 was on the horizon, and El Paso and Ciudad Juárez would find themselves at its very heart.

Fort Bliss in the Boomtown Years

As El Paso transformed into a boomtown in the late 19th century, Fort Bliss grew alongside it. Originally a modest outpost, by the 1880s the fort had become a permanent installation, relocated to its current site northeast of the city. Its presence was both stabilizing and disruptive.

- A stabilizing force: Soldiers from Fort Bliss patrolled the border, guarded against Apache raids, and provided a sense of order in a city notorious for saloons, gambling halls, and gunfights. Their uniforms and drills on the parade grounds were a reminder that the U.S. government's authority extended even to this wild frontier.

- An economic anchor: The fort's payroll supported local businesses. Merchants supplied food, uniforms, and equipment, while saloons and entertainment halls eagerly welcomed soldiers on leave.
- A cultural presence: The fort brought a steady stream of officers and enlisted men from across the United States, adding to El Paso's cosmopolitan mix of Anglos, Mexicans, and immigrants from Europe and Asia.

Yet Fort Bliss could not erase El Paso's reputation for lawlessness. Soldiers themselves sometimes contributed to the disorder, drinking and brawling in the city's saloons. The fort was both a symbol of order and a participant in the chaos of the boomtown years.

Preparing for a New Era

By the turn of the 20th century, Fort Bliss had become one of the most important military posts in the Southwest. Its strategic location on the border meant that it would inevitably play a central role in the upheavals soon to come. As revolution brewed in Mexico, the fort's garrison expanded, its mission shifting from frontier defense to international vigilance.

Chapter 10: Borderlands of Revolution

A Valley in Upheaval

In 1910, the valley of El Paso and Ciudad Juárez stood at the crossroads of history. On the Mexican side, discontent with the long dictatorship of Porfirio Díaz erupted into revolution. On the American side, El Paso was booming, its streets filled with merchants, railroad men, and new arrivals drawn by opportunity. The river that divided the two cities became a stage for revolution, refuge, and reinvention.

Revolution Across the River

The Mexican Revolution began in earnest when Francisco I. Madero called for rebellion against Díaz. Ciudad Juárez quickly became a focal point. In May 1911, revolutionary forces under Pancho Villa and Pascual Orozco laid siege to Juárez. The battle raged within sight of El Paso, and stray bullets even crossed the river, striking buildings and terrifying residents.

When Juárez fell to the revolutionaries, Díaz's regime collapsed, and Madero became president. For El Pasoans, the revolution was not a distant war but a daily reality. Refugees poured across the river, revolutionaries plotted in El Paso saloons, and U.S. troops patrolled the border. The valley became a front-row seat to Mexico's upheaval, its streets alive with intrigue, espionage, and the constant hum of uncertainty.

El Paso as a Refuge and Stage

El Paso became a haven for exiles, journalists, and revolutionaries. Leaders like Madero, Villa, and Carranza all spent time in the city, using it as a base for organizing and fundraising. American businessmen, meanwhile, watched nervously as the revolution threatened their investments in Mexican mines and railroads.

The border was porous. Arms flowed south, refugees flowed north, and ideas flowed both ways. The revolution blurred the line between the two cities, binding them together in conflict and survival.

Fort Bliss and the Mexican Revolution

When the Mexican Revolution erupted in 1910, Fort Bliss became the nerve center of U.S. military operations along the border. Its soldiers were tasked with maintaining order in El Paso, monitoring the fighting across the river in Ciudad Juárez, and preparing for the possibility that the conflict might spill into U.S. territory.

- The Battle of Ciudad Juárez (1911): As Madero's forces besieged Juárez, U.S. troops from Fort Bliss lined the Rio Grande, protecting El Paso from stray fire and preventing American citizens from joining the fight. Despite their efforts, bullets crossed the river, striking buildings in El Paso and terrifying residents. The fort's presence reassured the city, even as it underscored the fragility of the border.
- Refugees and revolutionaries: Thousands of Mexican refugees fled north, many settling in El Paso under the watchful eye of Fort Bliss. At the same time, revolutionaries used the city as a base for organizing, often under the

surveillance of U.S. soldiers and intelligence officers.

• The Punitive Expedition (1916): After Pancho Villa's raid on Columbus, New Mexico, Fort Bliss became the staging ground for General John J. Pershing's Punitive Expedition into Mexico. Thousands of soldiers marched south from the fort, though Villa eluded capture. The expedition cemented Fort Bliss's role as a key military hub in U.S.–Mexico relations.

A Permanent Military Presence

By the 1920s, Fort Bliss was no longer a frontier outpost but a permanent institution. Its training grounds expanded, its garrison grew, and its influence on El Paso deepened. The fort provided jobs, stability, and a sense of national importance to a city that had once been dismissed as a lawless border town.

Gliding into Modern History

As El Paso built schools, universities, and civic institutions, Fort Bliss remained a constant presence. It was both a guardian and a reminder: the valley was not only a crossroads of cultures but also a frontier of nations, where the U.S. Army stood watch.

The fort's story glided seamlessly into the era of revolution, depression, and war. In the decades to come, it would expand into one of the largest military installations in the United States, shaping El Paso's destiny as much as the river or the railroad.

Building a Future Amidst Chaos: Education in El Paso

Even as revolution shook Mexico, El Paso was laying the foundations of its future through education.

- 1913: The Founding of UTEP
In 1913, the Texas State School of Mines and Metallurgy was established in El Paso, the institution that would later become the University of Texas at El Paso (UTEP). Its creation reflected the region's mining wealth and the need for trained engineers. The school's Bhutanese-style architecture, adopted in the 1910s, gave it a distinctive identity that endures today.
- 1916: El Paso High School

Just three years later, in 1916, El Paso High School opened its doors. Perched on a hill overlooking the city, its grand Greco-Roman architecture earned it the nickname "The Lady on the Hill." It became a symbol of civic pride, offering education to a rapidly growing population and anchoring El Paso's identity as a modern American city.

Between Boom and Bust

The 1920s brought prosperity to El Paso. The city thrived as a hub of trade, immigration, and culture. Prohibition in the United States sent Americans flocking across the river to Ciudad Juárez, where alcohol, gambling, and entertainment flourished. The two cities shared an economy of vice and vitality, each feeding the other's growth.

Yet beneath the prosperity, cracks were forming. The agricultural economy was fragile, dependent on cotton and migrant labor. Inequality persisted, and the city's rapid growth strained its infrastructure.

1929–1930: Austin High School and the Shadow of Depression

On the eve of the Great Depression, El Paso continued to invest in education. In 1929–1930, the city opened its second major high school, Austin High School, to serve the expanding population in the city's northeast. Its founding reflected both optimism and necessity — a belief that education was the key to stability in uncertain times.

But the optimism was short-lived. The stock market crash of 1929 and the economic collapse that followed hit El Paso hard. Trade slowed, jobs vanished, and the city's reliance on cross-border commerce was tested as never before.

A Borderland Identity Forged

By 1930, the valley had lived through revolution, boom, and the first tremors of depression. El Paso and Ciudad Juárez were no longer frontier towns but modern border cities, their destinies intertwined. The revolution had shown how events in Mexico could reshape life in Texas, while the growth of schools and institutions in El Paso reflected a determination to build a future even in the shadow of turmoil.

The border was both a line of division and a thread of connection. In the early 20th century, it was clearer than ever: the two cities would rise and fall together, sharing a destiny shaped by revolution, education, and resilience.

Chapter 11: Hard Times on the Border

The Great Depression Arrives

The stock market crash of 1929 reverberated across the nation, and El Paso was no exception. The city, which had grown rapidly in the 1920s, suddenly faced unemployment, shuttered businesses, and shrinking trade. Cotton prices collapsed, rail traffic slowed, and cross-border commerce with Ciudad Juárez faltered.

For many families, survival meant tightening belts, taking in boarders, or sending children to work. Mexican and Mexican-American laborers were hit especially hard. In the early 1930s, repatriation campaigns pressured thousands of Mexican families — many of them long-time residents or U.S. citizens — to leave El Paso and return to Mexico. The valley's population shifted, its wounds deepened by economic and social strain.

Fort Bliss as a Lifeline

Amid the hardship, Fort Bliss provided a measure of stability. Though the Army itself faced budget cuts during the Depression, the fort remained a steady employer and consumer of local goods. Soldiers' paychecks circulated through El Paso's shops, saloons, and markets, keeping the city's economy from collapsing entirely.

- Employment anchor: Civilian workers found jobs at the fort as clerks, cooks, and laborers. For many families, these wages were the difference between hunger and survival.
- Military presence: The fort's garrison, though modest, reassured El Pasoans that the city remained strategically important. Even in lean years, the Army could not abandon its post on the border.
- Community ties: Soldiers and their families became part of El Paso's fabric, attending local churches, schools, and civic events. The fort was not just a military installation — it was a community within a community.

Civic Growth in Lean Years

Despite the Depression, El Paso continued to invest in its future. The city's schools, including El Paso High School (1916) and Austin High School (1929/1930), became symbols of resilience, educating a new generation even as families struggled. The Texas College of Mines and Metallurgy (UTEP), founded in 1913, expanded slowly, training engineers who would one day serve both industry and the military.

Public works projects, funded by New Deal programs, brought jobs and improvements: new roads, schools, and civic buildings. These projects gave El Pasoans a sense of progress amid hardship, and they tied the city more closely to the federal government — a relationship mirrored in the presence of Fort Bliss.

Ciudad Juárez Across the River

On the south bank, Ciudad Juárez weathered the Depression differently. Mexico's economy was less tied to Wall Street, but Juárez felt the effects of reduced cross-border trade. Yet the city also benefited from Prohibition's lingering shadow: Americans continued to cross the river for entertainment, alcohol, and gambling, providing Juárez with a steady stream of revenue.

The two cities leaned on one another, as they always had. When El Paso faltered, Juárez offered escape; when Juárez struggled, El Paso's markets provided goods. The river was a border, but survival was shared.

Fort Bliss Expands Again

By the late 1930s, as the world edged toward war, Fort Bliss began to grow once more. The Army recognized the fort's strategic location — close to Mexico, near vital rail lines, and with ample desert land for training.

- Anti-aircraft training: Fort Bliss became a center for anti-aircraft artillery, preparing soldiers for the modern warfare that loomed on the horizon.
- Infrastructure improvements: New barracks, training grounds, and facilities were built, bringing construction jobs and federal dollars into El Paso.
- Foreshadowing war: Soldiers drilled in the desert sun, their exercises a reminder that the world beyond the valley was growing more dangerous by the day.

December 7, 1941: A World Transformed

On a quiet Sunday morning, news crackled across radios in El Paso: Pearl Harbor had been attacked. The United States was at war.

For El Paso and Fort Bliss, the announcement was both shocking and galvanizing. Within hours, soldiers were mobilized, families braced for separation, and the city prepared for a wartime economy. The Depression years, with their hardship and uncertainty, were suddenly behind them. Ahead lay a new era of sacrifice, mobilization, and transformation.

The valley that had endured revolution, boomtown chaos, and economic collapse was now thrust onto the global stage. Fort Bliss would expand into one of the largest military installations in the country, and El Paso would become a city defined not by survival alone, but by its role in a world at war.

Chapter 12: A City at War

Mobilizing the Borderlands

The attack on Pearl Harbor in December 1941 thrust the United States into World War II, and El Paso felt the shock immediately. The city that had weathered the Great Depression now found itself on the front lines of mobilization. Factories, railroads, and civic institutions shifted to wartime footing, and Fort Bliss—already a significant military post—expanded at a pace never before seen.

The desert that had once been a quiet training ground became a hive of activity. Soldiers poured in from across the nation, convoys rumbled through the streets, and the sound of marching boots and artillery drills echoed across the valley.

Fort Bliss: From Outpost to Powerhouse

Fort Bliss had been important before, but World War II transformed it into one of the largest military installations in the United States.

- Anti-Aircraft Artillery Training: Fort Bliss became the Army's premier center for anti-aircraft training. Thousands of soldiers learned to operate searchlights, radar, and heavy guns designed to protect cities and bases from enemy aircraft.
- Massive Expansion: The base sprawled outward, consuming desert land for new barracks, motor pools, and training ranges. Civilian contractors and local workers found steady employment building the infrastructure of war.
- Community Impact: The influx of soldiers and their families swelled El Paso's population, straining housing and services but also fueling economic growth. Restaurants, shops, and theaters thrived on military paychecks.

Biggs Army Airfield: The Aviation Frontier

Alongside Fort Bliss, aviation became central to the war effort. The aviation field at Fort

Bliss, originally a modest landing strip, was expanded and renamed Biggs Army Airfield.

- Strategic Role: Biggs became a key training site for bomber crews and transport pilots. Its wide runways and desert climate made it ideal for year-round flying.
- Aircraft Operations: Heavy bombers, including B-17 Flying Fortresses and later B-24 Liberators, used Biggs for training missions. Transport planes ferried men and supplies across the Southwest, preparing for deployment overseas.
- Integration with Fort Bliss: The airfield worked hand-in-hand with the Army's ground training. Anti-aircraft gunners at Fort Bliss practiced against aircraft flying from Biggs, creating a combined-arms training environment that mirrored the realities of modern war.

El Paso: A Wartime City

The war reshaped El Paso itself.

- Population Surge: The city's population grew rapidly as soldiers, defense workers, and

their families arrived. Schools, hospitals, and housing developments struggled to keep pace.
- Women in the Workforce: Like elsewhere in the nation, El Pasoan women stepped into roles once reserved for men, working in offices, factories, and even on the base.
- Cultural Exchange: The presence of soldiers from across the country brought new accents, traditions, and ideas, blending with El Paso's already diverse mix of Mexican, Anglo, and Indigenous cultures.

The Border in Wartime

Across the river, Ciudad Juárez also felt the war's impact. Mexican workers crossed daily to labor in El Paso's industries, while the Bracero Program (1942) formalized the recruitment of Mexican laborers for U.S. farms and railroads. The two cities, already intertwined, became even more dependent on one another.

A City Transformed

By the end of World War II, El Paso was no longer the dusty frontier town of the 19th century. It was a modern military city, anchored by Fort Bliss and Biggs Army Airfield. The war had brought prosperity, diversity, and growth, but also a new identity: El Paso was now inseparable from the U.S. Army's mission.

The desert had become a proving ground for modern warfare, and the city had become a community defined by its role in a global struggle. The war would end in 1945, but its legacy would shape El Paso and Fort Bliss for decades to come.

Chapter 13: The Cold War Frontier

A New World Order

The end of World War II in 1945 brought victory but also uncertainty. The United States emerged as a superpower, locked in ideological and military rivalry with the Soviet Union. For El Paso and its military installations, the Cold War meant transformation. The desert frontier became a frontline of preparation, where soldiers trained not for distant battlefields alone but for the defense of the homeland itself.

Fort Bliss: The Missile Era

During the Cold War, Fort Bliss evolved from an artillery training post into one of the most important missile and air defense centers in the United States.

- German Rocket Scientists: After the war, under Operation Paperclip, German scientists who had worked on the V-2 rocket were brought to the U.S. Some were stationed at Fort Bliss in the late 1940s, where they tested and refined rocket technology in the desert.

This marked the beginning of El Paso's role in the space and missile age.

• Anti-Aircraft to Air Defense: Fort Bliss shifted from traditional anti-aircraft artillery to training soldiers on the new generation of guided missiles. The Nike missile program and later the Patriot missile system made the fort a cornerstone of America's air defense strategy.

• Expansion of Training Grounds: The fort's ranges sprawled across the desert, providing vast space for live-fire exercises and missile testing. Thousands of soldiers cycled through Fort Bliss, learning to operate the weapons that would defend American cities from potential Soviet bombers.

Biggs Army Airfield: Strategic Aviation

Next door, Biggs Army Airfield also expanded during the Cold War.

• Strategic Air Command (SAC): In the 1950s, Biggs became a base for SAC bombers, including the B-36 Peacemaker and later the B-52 Stratofortress. These massive aircraft,

capable of carrying nuclear weapons, symbolized America's deterrent power.
• Global Reach: From Biggs, bombers could reach targets across the globe. The airfield's runways were lengthened to accommodate the largest aircraft of the era, making it one of the most important SAC bases in the Southwest.
• Transition: By the 1960s, SAC operations shifted elsewhere, and Biggs was eventually transferred to the Army, becoming Biggs Army Airfield once again, integrated with Fort Bliss's mission.

El Paso: A City Shaped by the Cold War

The Cold War military buildup reshaped El Paso itself.

• Population Growth: Soldiers and their families poured into the city, swelling its population and fueling demand for housing, schools, and services.
• Economic Dependence: Fort Bliss and Biggs became the city's economic anchors. Local businesses thrived on military contracts, and

the steady flow of federal dollars insulated El Paso from some of the economic turbulence that hit other regions.
- Cultural Exchange: The presence of soldiers from across the nation — and later, international trainees from allied countries — made El Paso a crossroads of cultures, blending its Mexican-American heritage with influences from across the globe.

The Border in the Cold War

The U.S.–Mexico border also took on new significance. While El Paso and Ciudad Juárez remained deeply interconnected, the Cold War heightened concerns about security and surveillance. The river was no longer just a line between nations but a monitored frontier in a world divided by ideology.

At the same time, the Bracero Program (1942–1964) continued to bring Mexican laborers into the U.S., many of them passing through El Paso. The city became a gateway not only for soldiers and missiles but also for workers whose labor sustained American agriculture and industry.

A Frontier of the Future

By the 1970s and 1980s, Fort Bliss had become synonymous with missile defense. The fort trained soldiers from NATO and allied nations, making El Paso an international military hub. Biggs Army Airfield supported these missions, while the city itself grew into a modern urban center, its skyline rising against the Franklin Mountains.

The Cold War frontier was not marked by battles in El Paso, but by preparation, vigilance, and transformation. The desert that had once echoed with the chants of friars and the gunfire of revolutionaries now thundered with the roar of jet engines and the launch of missiles.

A German Presence in the Desert

In January 1956, the desert city of El Paso became home to an unexpected new community: the German Air Force. As part of NATO cooperation during the Cold War, the German Air Force Air Defense School was established at Fort Bliss, bringing hundreds of

German officers, enlisted personnel, and their families to the borderlands.

This was no small gesture. Barely a decade earlier, the United States and Germany had been enemies in World War II. Now, in the face of the Soviet threat, they stood as allies. The decision to host German forces in El Paso symbolized not only reconciliation but also the global reach of the Cold War.

Training for a New Era of Warfare

The German Air Force Air Defense School focused on missile and anti-aircraft training, reflecting the shift from conventional artillery to advanced air defense systems.

- Shared Technology: German personnel trained on the same missile systems as their American counterparts, including the Nike Hercules and later the Patriot missile system.
- Joint Exercises: German and American soldiers drilled side by side in the desert ranges, forging bonds that transcended language and nationality.
- Innovation Hub: The school became a center of technical expertise, where NATO

allies exchanged knowledge and tactics in preparation for the possibility of Soviet air attacks.

An International Community in El Paso

The arrival of German families gave El Paso a new international flavor.

• Cultural Exchange: German children attended local schools, German families shopped in El Paso's markets, and friendships blossomed across cultures. Oktoberfest celebrations, German bakeries, and cultural clubs added new traditions to the city's already diverse identity.
• Economic Impact: The presence of German personnel boosted the local economy, as they rented homes, bought goods, and participated in civic life.
• Diplomatic Symbolism: For El Pasoans, the German presence was a daily reminder that their city was not just a border town but a node in a global alliance.

Fort Bliss as a NATO Hub

With the German Air Force Air Defense School, Fort Bliss became more than a U.S. Army post — it became a NATO training center. Soldiers from across the Atlantic trained in the Texas desert, preparing for a war that, if it came, would be fought in Europe but defended from everywhere.

This gave El Paso a unique role in the Cold War: it was both a local city on the U.S.–Mexico border and an international military hub, where the fates of nations converged.

A City with Global Reach

By the late 1950s and into the 1960s, El Paso's identity was firmly tied to its military presence. Fort Bliss trained U.S. and allied soldiers in missile defense. Biggs Army Airfield supported strategic aviation. And the German Air Force Air Defense School gave the city a distinctly international character.

El Paso was no longer just a frontier town or even just a border city. It was a Cold War frontier, where the desert became a proving ground for global defense, and where the presence of German soldiers and families underscored the city's role in a world divided between East and West.

The 1970s: A City and a Base Bound Together

By the 1970s, El Paso and Fort Bliss were no longer separate entities but interdependent partners. The city's economy, schools, and neighborhoods were shaped by the rhythms of the base, while Fort Bliss relied on El Paso for housing, services, and community life.

- Population Growth: El Paso's population surged past 300,000 by the mid-1970s, fueled in part by the steady presence of soldiers and their families. Entire neighborhoods — from the Northeast near the base to the West Side — grew to accommodate military families.
- Educational Expansion: The city invested heavily in schools to serve its growing youth population. New high schools such as Irvin High School (1959), Andress High School (1961), and later Parkland (1962) and Bowie's expansion reflected the demographic boom. By the 1970s and 1980s, El Paso's school system was one of the largest in Texas, with

Fort Bliss families making up a significant portion of enrollment.

- UTEP's Rise: The University of Texas at El Paso (UTEP), founded in 1913, expanded dramatically in these decades. Its programs in engineering and international studies drew on the city's military and borderland identity, while its Bhutanese-style campus became a cultural landmark. Many soldiers stationed at Fort Bliss took courses at UTEP, further linking the base and the university.

Fort Bliss: The Missile Capital of the Free World

During the late Cold War, Fort Bliss solidified its reputation as the Army's premier air defense training center.

- Patriot Missile System: In the 1980s, Fort Bliss became the home of training for the Patriot missile system, the most advanced air defense weapon of its time. Soldiers from across the U.S. and allied nations trained in El Paso's desert, preparing for the possibility of Soviet missile or aircraft attacks.

- International Training: The German Air Force Air Defense School, established in 1956, continued to thrive. By the 1970s and 1980s, thousands of German soldiers and their families had lived in El Paso, creating a lasting cultural exchange. German bakeries, Oktoberfest celebrations, and bilingual friendships became part of the city's fabric.
- NATO Presence: Beyond Germany, soldiers from other NATO allies also trained at Fort Bliss, giving El Paso a distinctly international character. Few American cities could claim such a global military presence.

Biggs Army Airfield: Supporting the Mission

Though Biggs had lost its role as a Strategic Air Command bomber base in the 1960s, it remained vital as Biggs Army Airfield, integrated with Fort Bliss.

- Logistics and Support: Biggs provided airlift capacity for troops and equipment, ensuring that Fort Bliss could project power rapidly.
- Training Integration: Aircraft flying from Biggs supported missile and air defense

training, creating a combined-arms environment that mirrored Cold War realities.
• Community Symbol: The roar of aircraft overhead became part of daily life in El Paso, a reminder that the city was tied to global defense.

El Paso: A Border City with Global Reach

By the 1980s, El Paso was no longer just a border town — it was a Cold War city.

• Economic Dependence: Fort Bliss and Biggs were the city's largest employers, directly or indirectly supporting tens of thousands of jobs.
• Cultural Exchange: The German presence, combined with soldiers from across the U.S., made El Paso one of the most diverse cities in Texas. Its identity was a blend of Mexican heritage, American military culture, and international influences.
• Education and Growth: New schools continued to open, reflecting the city's growth. The El Paso Independent School District and Ysleta ISD expanded campuses,

while UTEP grew into a respected research university.

The Cold War's Shadow

Even as El Paso thrived, the Cold War loomed large. The threat of nuclear war was never far from mind, and Fort Bliss's mission underscored the seriousness of the era. Soldiers trained daily for a conflict that everyone hoped would never come.

Yet in the process, the city and the base became inseparable. El Paso's economy, culture, and identity were tied to Fort Bliss and Biggs, while the base relied on the city for its vitality. Together, they formed a community that was both local and global, rooted in the desert but connected to the fate of the world.

Chapter 14: The Border in Transition

A Winter to Remember

In December 1987, El Paso experienced one of the most extraordinary weather events in its history: a record-setting snowfall that blanketed the desert city in white. More than a foot of snow fell, paralyzing traffic, closing schools, and transforming the Franklin Mountains into a winter landscape few had ever seen. For a city accustomed to sun and sand, the storm was both disruptive and magical — a reminder that even in the desert, history could surprise.

The snowstorm became a metaphor for the years ahead: unexpected, transformative, and unforgettable.

The End of the Cold War

As the 1980s drew to a close, the world shifted. The Berlin Wall fell in 1989, the Soviet Union dissolved in 1991, and the Cold War — the defining conflict of the 20th century — came to an end. For El Paso, Fort Bliss, and Biggs Army Airfield, this global transformation carried profound consequences.

- Fort Bliss's Mission Evolves: With the Soviet threat receding, the Army reassessed its priorities. Fort Bliss remained the Army's premier air defense training center, but its focus shifted from preparing for global nuclear

war to regional conflicts and peacekeeping missions.
- Biggs Army Airfield: Though no longer a Strategic Air Command base, Biggs continued to support Fort Bliss with transport and logistics, ensuring the post remained a vital hub for deployment and training.
- A City in Transition: El Paso, long defined by its role in the Cold War, now had to adapt to a world where the old enemy was gone but new uncertainties loomed.

The German Air Force's Departure

One of the most visible symbols of the Cold War in El Paso had been the German Air Force Air Defense School, established at Fort Bliss in 1956. For decades, German soldiers and their families had lived in the city, creating a unique cultural exchange.

- Departure in the 1990s: With the Cold War over and Germany reunified, the German Air Force gradually drew down its presence in El Paso. By the early 2000s, the school had closed, and the German mission shifted back to Europe.

- Legacy: The departure was bittersweet. El Pasoans had grown accustomed to their German neighbors, whose Oktoberfests, bakeries, and cultural clubs had enriched the city. The German presence left a lasting imprint, remembered fondly by those who had shared classrooms, neighborhoods, and friendships.

El Paso's Growth in a New Era

Even as the Cold War ended, El Paso continued to grow.

- Population Expansion: By the 1990s, El Paso's population surpassed 500,000, making it one of the largest cities in Texas.
- Economic Shifts: The city diversified its economy, with trade, manufacturing, and education joining the military as pillars of growth. The North American Free Trade Agreement (NAFTA), signed in 1994, further tied El Paso's fortunes to cross-border commerce with Ciudad Juárez.
- Fort Bliss as Anchor: Despite defense cutbacks nationwide, Fort Bliss remained a cornerstone of the city's identity. Its training mission, international reputation, and

economic impact ensured that El Paso would remain a military city even in a post-Cold War world.

Adapting to a Post-Cold War World

The 1990s were a decade of adjustment. The old certainties of the Cold War were gone, but El Paso adapted with resilience.

• Military-Civilian Partnership: The city and Fort Bliss deepened their ties, working together on housing, infrastructure, and education.
• Border Dynamics: Immigration, trade, and cross-border culture became central to El Paso's identity, as the city leaned into its role as a true binational community.
• A Global Outlook: Even without the German Air Force, El Paso retained its international character. Soldiers from allied nations continued to train at Fort Bliss, and the city's universities and businesses embraced their role in a globalizing world.

Conclusion: From Cold War to New Century

The record snowfall of the late 1980s had been a moment of wonder, a disruption that forced the city to adapt. The end of the Cold War was much the same: unexpected, transformative, and demanding resilience.

By the dawn of the 21st century, El Paso had emerged as a city that was both local and global, rooted in the desert but connected to the world. Fort Bliss remained its anchor, Biggs its aviation arm, and the memory of its German neighbors a reminder that history had made El Paso not just a border city, but a crossroads of nations.

Chapter 15: A New Century of War and Change

September 11, 2001: A Nation Transformed

On the morning of September 11, 2001, the United States was struck by terrorist attacks that killed thousands and shook the nation's sense of security. For El Paso, the shock was immediate and personal. Soldiers at Fort Bliss were placed on high alert, the base sealed under heightened security. Families gathered around televisions, knowing that the world had changed — and that their city, home to one of the Army's most important posts, would soon be drawn deeply into the wars to come.

Fort Bliss: From Regional Post to Global Powerhouse

In the years after 9/11, Fort Bliss underwent a massive expansion that reshaped both the base and the city of El Paso.

- Base Realignment and Closure (BRAC) 2005: The Department of Defense designated Fort Bliss as a major growth site. Thousands of soldiers and their families were relocated from other installations, including the 1st Armored Division from Germany.
- Population Surge: Fort Bliss grew from roughly 10,000 soldiers in the early 2000s to more than 30,000 by the 2010s, with tens of thousands of family members accompanying them. This made it one of the largest Army posts in the United States.
- Infrastructure Boom: Entire neighborhoods of new housing, schools, medical facilities, and training ranges were built. The base expanded across vast stretches of desert, creating one of the largest contiguous training areas in the country.

Training for the War on Terror

Fort Bliss became a central hub for preparing soldiers for the wars in Afghanistan and Iraq.

- Desert Training Grounds: The Chihuahuan Desert provided an ideal environment for simulating Middle Eastern terrain. Soldiers trained in mock villages, practiced convoy

operations, and drilled in counterinsurgency tactics.
- Air Defense and Beyond: While Fort Bliss remained the Army's premier air defense training center, its mission broadened to include armored warfare, infantry training, and joint operations.
- Deployment Cycles: Thousands of El Paso soldiers deployed overseas, while their families endured long separations. The city became a community of sacrifice, resilience, and support.

Biggs Army Airfield: A Strategic Hub

Biggs Army Airfield, integrated with Fort Bliss, also expanded its role.

- Deployment Gateway: Biggs became a major departure point for troops heading to the Middle East. Soldiers boarded transport planes bound for Kuwait, Afghanistan, and Iraq, with El Paso as their last glimpse of home.
- Logistics and Support: The airfield handled the movement of equipment, supplies, and personnel on a scale not seen since World War II.

El Paso: A City Transformed

The expansion of Fort Bliss reshaped El Paso itself.

• Economic Growth: The influx of soldiers and families fueled a construction boom, new businesses, and job creation. Restaurants, schools, and hospitals expanded to meet demand.
• Cultural Exchange: Soldiers from across the United States — and allied nations — brought new traditions, accents, and perspectives, adding to El Paso's already diverse identity.
• Challenges: The rapid growth strained infrastructure, from traffic to housing. Yet the city adapted, embracing its role as a military metropolis.

A Shared Destiny in a New Century

The attacks of 9/11 had changed the nation forever, and El Paso was no exception. Fort Bliss's expansion made the city a pillar of America's war effort, its desert ranges echoing with the sounds of training for conflicts half a world away.

For El Pasoans, the wars were not distant headlines. They were lived daily — in deployments, homecomings, and the ever-present awareness that their city was tied to the fate of soldiers fighting abroad.

By the end of the first decade of the 21st century, El Paso had become not just a border city, not just a Cold War outpost, but a global military hub, its destiny forever linked to the wars that followed September 11.

Chapter 16: A City of Soldiers and Families

The Human Face of Expansion

The massive expansion of Fort Bliss after 9/11 was not just about new barracks, training ranges, or aircraft. It was about people. Tens of thousands of soldiers and their families arrived in El Paso in the 2000s and 2010s, transforming the city's neighborhoods, schools, and culture.

For many, El Paso was their first posting, their first home away from home. For others, it was a place of return, a city where deployments began and ended. The rhythms of military life — deployments, homecomings, farewells, and reunions — became the rhythms of El Paso itself.

Deployments and Homecomings

The wars in Afghanistan and Iraq defined the decade.

- Deployments: Soldiers from Fort Bliss rotated overseas for months at a time.

Families endured long separations, with spouses raising children alone and communities rallying to support them.
- Homecomings: The return of units was marked by emotional reunions at Biggs Army Airfield. Families gathered with banners and tears, children ran into the arms of parents they hadn't seen in a year, and the city celebrated its heroes.
- Sacrifice: Not all came home. Memorials and ceremonies reminded El Paso that the cost of war was borne not only abroad but also in the hearts of families at home.

Families on the Frontline of Community

The expansion of Fort Bliss meant that military families became a central part of El Paso's identity.

- Schools: Thousands of military children enrolled in El Paso's public schools. Teachers adapted to the unique challenges of students who moved frequently or whose parents were deployed.

- Neighborhoods: Entire subdivisions sprang up near the base, filled with families who brought new energy and diversity to the city.
- Support Networks: Churches, nonprofits, and civic groups created programs for military spouses, veterans, and children, weaving the military community into the fabric of El Paso.

El Paso's Identity as a Military City

By the 2010s, El Paso was no longer just a border city — it was a military city.

- Economy: Fort Bliss became the largest employer in the region, its payroll sustaining businesses from restaurants to real estate.
- Culture: Military ceremonies, parades, and commemorations became part of the city's calendar. The sight of soldiers in uniform at the grocery store or in the stands at a UTEP football game became ordinary.
- Shared Destiny: The line between "civilian El Paso" and "military Fort Bliss" blurred. The two were no longer separate worlds but one community, bound by shared sacrifice and pride.

The 2000s and 2010s: A City Transformed

The human side of Fort Bliss's expansion reshaped El Paso in ways that statistics alone cannot capture.

- Resilience: Families learned to endure the uncertainty of war, leaning on one another and on the city for support.
- Diversity: Soldiers from across the United States — and allied nations — brought new traditions, accents, and perspectives, enriching El Paso's already multicultural identity.
- Pride: El Paso embraced its role as a city of soldiers and families, proud of its contribution to the nation's defense and aware of the sacrifices it entailed.

Inseparable Identities

By the end of the 2010s, El Paso's identity was inseparable from Fort Bliss. The city was no longer simply a host to a military base — it was a community of soldiers and families, where the rhythms of military life shaped the rhythms of civic life.

The desert had always been a place of endurance. In the 21st century, it became a place of resilience, where soldiers trained for wars abroad and families built lives at home, together forging a city defined by service, sacrifice, and strength.

Chapter 17: The Border in the 21st Century

A City at the Crossroads of Change

As the 21st century unfolded, El Paso found itself in a world transformed by technology, globalization, and shifting demographics. Once seen as a remote border town, El Paso was now recognized as a strategic city between both coasts of the United States, a place where east meets west and north meets south.

The city's identity — forged by centuries of resilience, migration, and military presence — was now being reshaped by new opportunities in trade, education, technology, and culture.

Technology and Transformation

The digital revolution reached the desert.

- Education and Research: The University of Texas at El Paso (UTEP) expanded its research programs, particularly in engineering, health sciences, and cross-border studies. Its

graduates entered fields that connected El Paso to global industries.
- Medical Advances: The creation of the Texas Tech University Health Sciences Center El Paso brought cutting-edge medical education and research to the city, making it a hub for healthcare in the borderlands.
- Innovation and Industry: Technology firms and logistics companies began to see El Paso as a gateway city, strategically located for trade with Mexico and beyond.

Trade and Opportunity

El Paso's location on the U.S.–Mexico border became more valuable than ever.

- NAFTA and Beyond: The North American Free Trade Agreement (1994) and its successor, the USMCA (2020), positioned El Paso as a vital node in continental trade. Goods flowed through the city's ports of entry, linking factories in Ciudad Juárez with markets across the United States.
- Logistics Hub: With its railroads, highways, and proximity to Mexico's maquiladora industry, El Paso became a logistics

powerhouse, connecting supply chains from coast to coast.
• Job Creation: Warehousing, transportation, and manufacturing provided new opportunities, even as the city worked to diversify its economy beyond the military and trade.

A Military Metropolis in a Modern World

Fort Bliss remained central to El Paso's identity, but its role evolved in the 21st century.

• Global Deployments: Soldiers trained in El Paso continued to serve in conflicts abroad, linking the city to global events.
• Community Integration: Military families became deeply woven into El Paso's neighborhoods, schools, and civic life.
• Technology and Defense: Fort Bliss embraced new technologies, from missile defense to drone operations, ensuring the city remained at the forefront of national security.

Culture, Dreams, and Identity

El Paso's cultural life flourished in the 21st century, reflecting its unique position as a binational, bicultural city.

- Arts and Music: Festivals, galleries, and music venues showcased the city's creativity, blending Mexican and American influences into something distinctly El Pasoan.
- Sports and Pride: UTEP athletics, the Sun Bowl, and professional soccer brought the community together, while the city's skyline and Franklin Mountains became symbols of pride.
- Dreams and Opportunities: For many, El Paso represented possibility — a place where immigrants built new lives, where students pursued education, and where families found community.

Balancing Tradition and Progress

The challenge of the 21st century was balance. El Paso had to honor its history while embracing change, preserve its cultural roots while welcoming innovation, and remain a border city while asserting its place on the national stage.

It succeeded by doing what it had always done: adapting. The same resilience that had carried the valley through empire, revolution, depression, and war now carried it into a new century.

A Vital City Between Coasts

By the 2010s and 2020s, El Paso was no longer seen as peripheral. It was a vital city between both coasts, a hub of trade, culture, and defense. Its location made it indispensable, its people made it vibrant, and its history made it strong.

El Paso was — and remains — a city of dreams and opportunities, where the desert meets the river, where nations meet, and where the future is written every day in the lives of its people.

Chapter 18: The Future of the Borderlands

A City Looking Forward

El Paso has always been a city of transformation. From mission outpost to boomtown, from Cold War frontier to military metropolis, it has continually adapted to the demands of history. Now, in the decades ahead, the challenge is not survival but **vision**: how to harness its unique position as a border city, a military hub, and a cultural crossroads to build a future of opportunity.

The Role of Leadership and Vision

The future of El Paso will depend on leadership that sees beyond the horizon. With the right vision, the city can continue to grow as a place where history and innovation meet.

- Strategic Planning: Leaders who invest in infrastructure, education, and healthcare will ensure that El Paso remains competitive in a rapidly changing world.
- Cross-Border Cooperation: Strong partnerships with Ciudad Juárez will allow the two cities to thrive together, leveraging their shared workforce, culture, and economy.

- Global Outlook: By embracing its role as a binational city, El Paso can position itself as a model for international cooperation in an era of globalization.

Healthcare as a Pillar of Growth

One of the greatest opportunities for El Paso lies in the expansion of medical facilities and research institutions.

- Medical Relocation and Expansion: With more hospitals, clinics, and specialized centers being built or relocated to El Paso, the city can become a healthcare hub for the entire Southwest.
- Texas Tech University Health Sciences Center El Paso: Already a cornerstone, it can grow into a world-class medical school and research institution, attracting talent and investment.
- Binational Healthcare: El Paso and Ciudad Juárez together can pioneer cross-border healthcare solutions, serving millions of people in the region and setting an example for international collaboration.

Technology, Trade, and Transformation

The decades ahead will also bring new opportunities in technology and trade.

- Logistics and Supply Chains: El Paso's location will remain vital as global trade routes shift. With investment in smart infrastructure, the city can become a leader in logistics and distribution.
- Technology and Innovation: Partnerships between UTEP, Fort Bliss, and private industry can foster innovation in defense, aerospace, and renewable energy.
- Sustainable Growth: With climate change reshaping the Southwest, El Paso can lead in water management, solar energy, and sustainable urban planning.

The Heart of Transformation

El Paso's greatest strength has always been its ability to meld worlds. It is a city where cultures, languages, and histories converge — and where the future can be written in harmony with the past.

- Cultural Identity: The city's binational heritage will remain its defining feature, a source of pride and creativity.
- Military and Civilian Unity: Fort Bliss will continue to anchor the city, ensuring that El Paso remains central to America's defense while enriching its civic life.
- Dreams and Opportunities: For immigrants, students, soldiers, and families, El Paso will remain a place where dreams take root and opportunities abound.

From the Pages of History to the Future

El Paso's story has always been one of resilience and reinvention. In the decades ahead, with the right leadership and vision, it can become not only the heart of the borderlands but also a beacon of transformation — a city that honors its past while shaping the future.

From the pages of history, El Paso has emerged as a place of endurance. In the future, it will stand as a place of possibility, where the desert becomes a canvas for innovation, and where the melding of worlds continues to define its destiny.

Epilogue: The Eternal Borderland

From the first adobe walls of the missions of El Paso del Norte, where friars planted vineyards and taught the faith along the Rio Grande, to the sprawling modern skyline that now rises against the Franklin Mountains, El Paso's story has always been one of endurance and transformation.

The valley has seen empires rise and fall. It has been Spanish, Mexican, and American. It has been a frontier outpost, a boomtown of saloons and railroads, a battlefield of revolution, and a Cold War stronghold. It has been a city of soldiers and families, of migrants and dreamers, of merchants and builders. Each chapter has left its mark, layering the city with a history as rich and complex as the desert soil itself.

Through it all, El Paso has never forgotten its roots. The missions still stand, their adobe walls whispering of faith and survival. The Rio Grande still flows, a reminder of the border that both divides and unites. The echoes of

Fort Bliss's parade grounds, the hum of trains, the laughter in plazas, and the prayers in churches all remind us that the past is never gone — it lives in the present.

And yet, El Paso is not a city bound by memory alone. It is a city of becoming. With each generation, it reinvents itself:

- From missions to railroads.
- From revolutions to universities.
- From Depression to wartime expansion.
- From Cold War vigilance to 21st-century innovation.

Looking forward, El Paso stands poised to be a city of the future — a hub of medicine, education, technology, and trade. Its binational character, once seen as a challenge, is now its greatest strength: a living example of how cultures can blend, how borders can connect, and how history can guide the future.

El Paso is the heart of the borderlands, a place where the desert teaches resilience, where the river teaches connection, and where the people — soldiers, families, immigrants, and dreamers — teach the world what it means to endure and to hope.

The story of El Paso is not finished. It is still being written in classrooms and barracks, in markets and laboratories, in homes on both sides of the river. It is a story that honors the past, embraces the present, and looks boldly toward the future.

For in El Paso, history is not a burden. It is a foundation. And on that foundation, the city will continue to rise — a place of dreams, opportunities, and transformation, forever shaped by its past, and forever reaching toward what lies ahead.

Made in the USA
Coppell, TX
29 November 2025

64268177R00077